Zion
National Park

John Hamilton

Published by ABDO Publishing Company, 8000 West 78th Street, Suite 310, Edina, MN 55439.
Copyright ©2009 by Abdo Consulting Group, Inc. International copyrights reserved in all countries.
No part of this book may be reproduced in any form without written permission from the publisher.
ABDO & Daughters™ is a trademark and logo of ABDO Publishing Company.

Printed in the United States.

Editor: Sue Hamilton
Graphic Design: John Hamilton
All photos and illustrations by the author, except National Park Service, p. 9 (Zion map), p. 26 (Kolob Arch) and p. 29 (firefighter).

Library of Congress Cataloging-in-Publication Data

Hamilton, John, 1959-
  Zion National Park / John Hamilton.
      p. cm. -- (National parks)
  Includes index.
  ISBN 978-1-60453-096-4
  1. Zion National Park (Utah)--Juvenile literature. I. Title.

F832.Z8H36 2009
979.2'48--dc22
                        2008011894

Contents

Left: The Virgin River flowing through Zion Canyon after an evening thunderstorm.

A hiker rests near Angels Landing overlooking Zion Canyon.

Canyons and Cliffs

Visiting Utah's Zion National Park is like being in the Grand Canyon in reverse. Just like Arizona's larger cousin, the canyons of Zion are steep-walled and majestic. But instead of standing on the canyon rim and looking down, visitors here enter at the bottom and look *up*. This neck craning provides a more awe-inspiring perspective. It lets viewers know just how small they are compared to the sandstone cliffs that tower above.

Nestled in the high plateau of southwest Utah, Zion National Park is a concentrated maze of deep canyons, mesas, forests, and streams. The park rests at the intersection of several large geologic regions: the Colorado Plateau, the Great Basin, and the Mojave Desert. Features and wildlife from all three regions are found in the park. There are several distinct ecosystems here, from desert in the south to forested highlands in the north. The variety of plant and animal life is also diverse, ranging from mountain lions and cottonwoods, to cactuses and tarantulas.

By far Zion's most striking appeal, the main reason it was set aside as a national park in 1919, are the many gorges and sandstone mesas. The colors of the rocks seem lifted directly from an artist's pallet. When touched by dawn or dusk sunlight, the rocks seem to glow red and yellow from within. Rivers cutting through the park produce narrow corridors of green, contrasting with the cliffs and desert landscape. In autumn, when the leaves change, a riot of colors erupts. In winter, a quiet hush settles over the park, wrapped in a blanket of white in the upper elevations.

Zion National Park isn't just for nature lovers; it's also a home for adventurers. Zion has more than 120 miles (193 km) of trails that wander through 229 square miles (593 sq km) of parkland. The trails range from easy, paved paths through tree-shaded riversides, to heart-pounding treks up sandstone bluffs hundreds of feet above the canyon floor. On some trails, such as a trip through The Narrows, hikers follow stream paths through narrow slot canyons. In fact, in The Narrows, the shallow river *is* the trail. Some routes transport visitors through gorges so narrow that sunlight seldom touches the canyon floor, and opposing cliff walls can be touched with outstretched arms.

Rock climbers come from all over the country to scramble over Zion's sandstone pillars. There's an abundance of free-climbing opportunities in the park, as well as several established harder routes. Popular walls include Spaceshot, Moonlight Buttress, and Touchstone.

For people seeking hard-core adventure, Zion's canyoneering is some of the best in the world. With about 50 technical canyons in the park, including Mystery Canyon and Pine Creek, eager explorers rappel down the park's red sandstone cliff walls into narrows and potholes that require special gear and training to escape.

Exploring Zion isn't limited to thrill seekers, however, although even the most tame activities can give visitors chills, thanks to the breathtaking canyon scenery. Besides the miles of easy trails available, tourists can take guided horseback rides into the roadless interior of the park. For bicyclists, the Pa'rus Trail is an easy, paved 3.5-mile (5.6-km) roundtrip through forested glens along the Virgin River to the entrance of Zion Canyon. Many people are content simply to sit and watch the ever-changing light on the canyon walls as the sun shifts across the desert sky. In Zion National Park, there is truly something for everyone.

Left: Zion's sandstone cliffs are a magnet for rock climbers and hikers looking for adventure.

Hikers make a steep ascent toward Angels Landing.

Sand, Wind, and Water

Zion National Park rests in Utah's desert country, along the edge of the Colorado Plateau. It's strange, then, that most of what is seen here was created by water. The park is in the middle of what is called the Grand Staircase, a series of cliffs stretching from Utah's Bryce Canyon National Park at the top, to Zion, to Arizona's Grand Canyon National Park at the bottom.

The Grand Staircase is made of great slabs of sedimentary rock. Millions of years ago, ancient oceans, deserts, and volcanoes deposited massive amounts of sand, mud, and ash. These sediments piled up until the immense pressure turned the layers to stone. Then, over millions of years, forces under the earth heaved the sandstone upward, as high as 10,000 feet (3,048 m) above sea level in some places. Wind, rain, and rivers etched the landscape, loosening the stone and carving the canyons we see today. This entire process took millions of years to complete, and is still going on. Every rain shower, every stream, and every windy day creates changes in Zion's landscape. As recently as 1992, an earthquake caused a landslide that altered the appearance of a hillside by the south entrance of the park near Springdale, Utah.

The waterway that cut Zion Canyon, the main attraction at the center of the park, is the north fork of the Virgin River. Over millions of years, the river cut through the rocks, revealing layers upon layers of geologic history. Zion contains many different kinds of rocks. Navajo sandstone is very colorful, with glowing reds and yellows. Its sweeping lines reveal the edges of ancient sand dunes. Kayenta mudstone, also common in the park, often contains the tracks of dinosaurs.

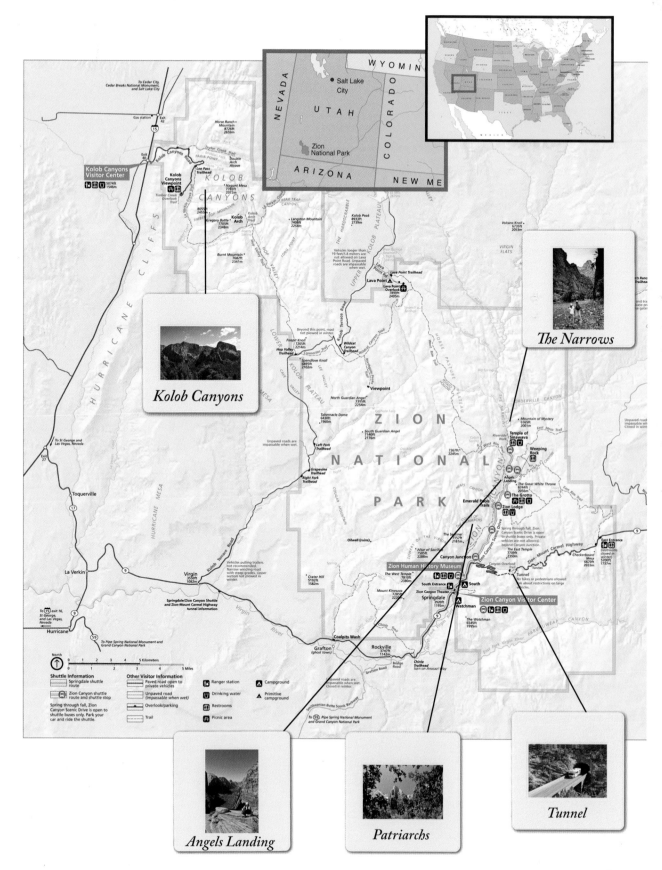

To Cedar City,
Cedar Breaks National Monument,
and Salt Lake City

Gas station

**Kolob Canyons
Visitor Center**
5074ft
1546m

Exit 42

Exit 40

Exit 27

To St George and
Las Vegas, Nevada

Toquerville

La Verkin

Hurricane

To 15 exit 16,
St George,
and Las Vegas,
Nevada

**Kolob
Canyons
Viewpoint**

*Horse Ranch
Mountain
8726ft
2659m*

Lee Pass
Trailhead

Taylor Creek Trail

*Double
Arch
Alcove*

K O L O B

Timber Top
Overlook Trail

*Nagunt Mesa
7785ft
2372m*

8055ft
2455m

**Kolob
Arch**

*Gregory Butte
7705ft
2348m*

Kolob
Arch
Trail

*Burnt Mountain
7682ft
2341m*

C A N Y O N S

*Langston Mountain
7406ft
2258m*

THE HARDSCRABBLE

**Kolob Peak
8933ft
2739m**

Vehicles longer than
19 feet/5.8 meters are
not allowed on Lava
Point Road. Unpaved
roads are impassable
when wet.

Beyond this point,
road not plowed in winter.

Firecat Knoll
7265ft
2214m

Hop Valley
Trailhead

*Spendlove Knoll
6895ft
2102m*

North Guardian Angel
3395ft
2254m

Tabernacle Dome
6430ft
1960m

*South Guardian Angel
7140ft
2176m*

Left Fork
Trailhead

Unpaved roads are
impassable when wet.

Grapevine
Trailhead

Right Fork
Trailhead

Oilwell (ruins)

Virgin
3550ft
1082m

Vehicles pulling trailers
not recommended.
Narrow winding road
with steep grades. Upper
section not plowed in
winter.

Springdale/Zion Canyon Shuttle
and Zion-Mount Carmel Highway
tunnel information

Crater Hill
5192ft
1582m

Coalpits Wash

Grafton
(ghost town)

Rockville
3747ft
1142m

To Pipe Spring National Monument and
Grand Canyon National Park

Grafton Road

Bridge
Road

Chinle
turn on Anasazi Way

To 59 Pipe Spring National Monument
and Grand Canyon National Park

Smithsonian Butte Scenic Backway

Lava Point
Trailhead

Lava Point

Lava Point
Overlook
2405m

Wildcat
Canyon
Trailhead

Viewpoint

Z I O N

N A T I O N A L

P A R K

*Volcano Knoll
6735ft
2053m*

**VIRGIN
FLATS**

Mountain of Mystery
6565ft
2001m

Temple of
Sinawava

Riverside
Walk

Weeping
Rock

*The Great White Throne
6744ft
2056m*

Angels
Landing

Emerald Pools
Trails

**Zion
Lodge**

The Grotto

*7367ft
2245m*

The Sentinel
7157ft
2181m

Altar of Sacrifice
7505ft
2288m

Spring through fall, Zion
Canyon Scenic Drive is open
to shuttle buses only. Private
vehicles are not allowed
beyond Canyon Junction.

Canyon Junction

Zion Human History Museum

*The West Temple
7810ft
2380m*

South Entrance

South

*The East Temple
7810ft
2380m*

Checkerboard
Mesa
6670ft
2033m

**East
Entrance**
restrooms
closed in
winter
5700ft
1737m

Tunnel

No bikes or pedestrians allowed
in tunnel. Ask about restrictions on large
vehicles.

Canyon Overlook

Zion Canyon Theater

Springdale
3920ft
1195m

Watchman

Zion Canyon Visitor Center

*The Watchman
6545ft
1995m*

Mount Kinesava
7285ft
2220m

North

Unpaved roads are
impassable when wet,
closed in winter.

0 1 2 3 4 5 Kilometers
0 1 2 3 4 5 Miles

Shuttle Information
Springdale shuttle
route

Zion Canyon shuttle
route and shuttle stop

Spring through fall, Zion
Canyon Scenic Drive is open to
shuttle buses only. Park your
car and ride the shuttle.

Other Visitor Information
Paved road open to
private vehicles

Unpaved road
(impassable when wet)

Overlook/parking

Trail

Ranger station

Drinking water

Restrooms

Picnic area

Campground

Primitive
campground

HURRICANE CLIFFS

HURRICANE MESA

Kolob Terrace Road

LOWER KOLOB PLATEAU

HOP VALLEY

LEE VALLEY

Connector Trail

COUGAR MOUNTAIN

Virgin River

The Narrows

Kolob Canyons

Angels Landing

Patriarchs

Tunnel

WYOMING

NEVADA

UTAH

Salt Lake
City

Zion
National Park

COLORADO

ARIZONA

NEW ME

9

The red and yellow cliffs of Zion National Park are made of Sandstone.

Flash Flood!

Although beautiful, the narrow canyons of Zion National Park must be treated with respect. Because the surrounding land is bare rock that doesn't absorb much rainwater, passing thunderstorms can bring life-threatening flash floods roaring down the canyons. Even falling rain many miles away can funnel down canyon walls, eventually reaching the park in a raging torrent.

The Narrows, as part of the north fork of the Virgin River, is very susceptible to flash flooding. Flash floods can strike without warning, especially during the late-summer/early-fall storm season. If you are hiking through a narrow slot canyon, be on the lookout for rising water levels, or a roaring sound up-canyon. Dangerous water levels can occur in a matter of minutes, or even seconds.

Always check with a park ranger before attempting a canyon hike. Weather forecasts are posted at park visitor centers. If you are caught in a flash flood, seek higher ground immediately. A human body is no match for the powerful wall of water and debris of a flash flood.

A dangerous Flash Flood surges through Coalpits Wash after a thunderstorm.

12 *"One hardly knows just how to think of it... this Great Temple of eternity."*

—Frederick S. Dellenbaugh, artist and explorer. *(Above: Angels Landing)* 13

History in the Park

The Crawford Ranch

Human history in the park goes back at least 12,000 years. Early Native Americans first came to the area to track mammoths and giant sloths. Overhunting and climate change caused these animals to die out about 8,000 years ago. Over the next several thousand years, native people called the Anasazi adapted to life in the area by hunting smaller animals and farming.

Because of drought and overuse, the Anasazi moved out of the area 800 years ago. They were eventually replaced by Paiute Native Americans. These desert dwellers thrived in Zion. They had a great respect for the canyon walls and sandstone monoliths, believing they were responsible for the life-giving streams and water the Paiute depended on. Today, there are many archaeological treasures found in the park, including ancient corn-storage jars, that remind us of these early people and their influence over the land.

In the late 18th century, the southern Utah area began to be explored and settled by European Americans. First to visit the area were Spanish explorers Padres Silvestre Vélez de Escalante and Francisco Atanasio Domínguez in 1776. In 1826, the area was explored by mountain man Jedediah Smith on his way to California.

The first white settlers in the Zion area were Mormon farmers who arrived in the 1850s and 1860s. They also raised livestock and prospected for minerals. These pioneers endured many hardships, including flash floods that destroyed entire towns.

In the early 1900s, people recognized the need to protect and preserve the area. Zion National Park was established on November 19, 1919. At first, travel to Zion was difficult, but after roads and a railroad line were built, tourism gained steadily, increasing the popularity of this special place.

How Zion Got Its Name

When Mormon pioneers first came to southern Utah in the mid-1800s, they were looking for a place to raise their families in peace, free from religious persecution. The flood plains along the Virgin River, south of Zion Canyon, seemed like a good choice. The area was suitable for farming and raising cattle, and was remote enough that the Mormons were generally left alone. Isaac Behunin, a farmer who settled in the area in 1863, is usually credited with giving Zion its name. Zion is a reference to a place named in the Bible, a place of refuge and peace.

Although the Mormons found great beauty in Zion, the area never really lived up to its name. Droughts and frequent floods made life difficult, often unbearable, for the pioneers.

In 1916, a Methodist minister named Frederick Vining Fisher took a trip to Zion. He was so awestruck by the sandstone monoliths and canyons that he named many of them after religious symbols. The names stuck, and today they are familiar sites inside the park: the Three Patriarchs, Angels Landing, the Organ, and the Great White Throne.

The Great White Throne in Zion Canyon.

Zion's Many Habitats

Zion is truly a land of diversity. Despite its location in Utah's arid southwest, Zion has such a varied elevation, between 3,650 and 8,725 feet (1,113 and 2,659 m), that several distinct life zones can be found inside the park. Water, or the lack of it, decides what lives, and where. At high elevations, on the plateau above the canyon rim, annual rainfall might average 26 inches (66 cm). The environment is cool and moist. White fir, ponderosa pine, quaking aspen, elk, and even peregrine falcons make their home there. In fact, more than 270 kinds of birds fly through Zion each year.

By contrast, at low elevations along canyon floors, especially canyons that open to the south and the beating sun, annual rainfall might total only 14 inches (36 cm). In this arid environment, Mojave Desert species scratch for survival, including sagebrush, cactus, desert tortoises, lizards, kangaroo rats, and tarantulas.

The real magic of Zion's habitats is in its riparian, or wetland, ecosystem. The waters of the Virgin River, which run all year long, give life to 500 times more species than exist in the surrounding desert. Even in summer heat—commonly 100 degrees Fahrenheit (38° C) or more—delicate, water-dependent species thrive in and along the shores of Zion's streams and rivers. Congregating along the park's water sources are cottonwood trees, box elder, scarlet monkeyflower, and golden columbine. Canyon treefrogs croak during the evening hours, always under the keen eyes of great blue herons hunting along the riverbeds. And living only in the lush ferns of the park's hanging gardens is the rare Zion snail.

Clumps of cactus grow along a canyon ridge (above). Much of Zion is arid desert. The park's wetlands, however, support a wide variety of plants and animals (below).

Zion Canyon

For most people, a trip to Zion means a drive up the main canyon road. Many arrive at the south entrance of the park from cities like nearby Salt Lake City, Utah, or Las Vegas, Nevada. The Zion Canyon Visitor Center is located on the outskirts of the tidy little town of Springdale, just outside the park entrance.

Heading north into Zion Canyon, great sandstone walls loom overhead on either side of the road. The Zion Human History Museum is just beyond the park entrance. It tells the story of the park's discovery and settlement, by both Native Americans and European Americans, through exhibits, photographs, and videos.

Starting at Canyon Junction, cars are not allowed on Zion Canyon Scenic Drive during busy summer months. Instead, propane-powered shuttle busses whisk visitors up the canyon free of charge. The road roughly follows the winding north fork of the Virgin River. Shade trees and the canyon walls themselves shield much of the canyon floor from the hot sun, except during midday. It's a pleasant experience to just sit back and relax, listening to the driver's narration as the bus quietly rolls past points of interest. There are several stops along the seven-mile (11-km) drive. Visitors are encouraged to get out, explore, and then hop on the next bus, which will take them deeper into the canyon.

Bus stop

The average width of Zion Canyon is just half a mile (.8 km). The canyon walls on either side soar 2,000 to 3,000 feet (610 to 914 m) high, giving the impression of walking through silent rows of skyscrapers. The Three Patriarchs is a famous trio of Navajo sandstone monoliths easily viewed from the road, or from a short trail to a viewing area called the Court of the Patriarchs Viewpoint.

Zion Canyon (above) was carved over a period of millions of years by the Virgin River.
The Three Patriarchs (below), from left to right: Abraham, Isaac, and Jacob.

One popular hike, just across the river from Zion Lodge, is the Emerald Pools Trail. The path is paved to prevent erosion. It leads to a natural rock basin that collects water from several streams. Maple trees provide shade as waterfalls gently mist the path, like a magical oasis in the desert. Moss grows from the side of the cliffs, and canyon treefrogs can often be heard croaking in the evening. Back at rustic Zion Lodge, which was rebuilt in 1966 after fire destroyed the original 1920s-era building, weary hikers can be found cooling off under shade trees, sipping water or eating ice cream cones.

For the more adventurous, there are several paths that lead up into canyon country. One of the most popular is the trek up to Angels Landing, a sandstone monolith that juts into the canyon like a thumb. A 2.5-mile (4-km) trail climbs more than 1,500 feet (457 m) to the top (see photo on pages 12-13). A marvel of engineering, the path was cut into the solid rock in 1926. In one short section, 21 switchbacks called "Walters Wiggles" take hikers almost straight up. The Angels Landing hike takes about three to four hours to complete. It is not for young children, or anyone afraid of heights. In places, sheer drops on either side of the narrow path drop 1,000 feet (305 m) or more. The hike can be a heart-pounding challenge, but the views from the top are spectacular, with Zion Canyon laid out far below in all its splendor.

Back on the shuttle bus, visitors can travel even farther up the canyon, with stops to explore hanging gardens such as Weeping Rock. The Great White Throne, a remarkable white sandstone monolith with streaks of red, rises 2,500 feet (762 m) above the canyon floor.

Left: Hikers trudge up Walters Wiggles, a steep series of switchbacks along the trail to Angels Landing.

Waterfalls splash into Emerald Pools (above), a cool oasis inside Zion Canyon. A path along the Angels Landing trail (below), with 1,000-foot (305-m) drops on either side.

The road ends at the Temple of Sinawava, a clearing named after the coyote spirit of the Paiute Native Americans. Here the canyon narrows. An easy two-mile (3.2-km) roundtrip path called the Riverside Walk provides a taste of Zion's wetland ecosystem. The mostly shaded walk takes visitors past hanging gardens of ferns and through groves of cottonwood and ash trees that grow along the Virgin River.

The Narrows begin at the end of Riverside Walk. Here the canyon walls constrict; in some places they are less than 20 feet (6 m) apart, yet soar higher than 2,000 feet (610 m). There is no path through The Narrows. Explorers must wade through the cold, ankle-deep waters of the Virgin River to see what's around the next bend. In some spots, the water deepens, requiring a short swim. It's a magical, awe-inspiring journey. However, if you decide to wander deep into the canyon, beware of flash floods. Always check for current weather conditions and ask about any travel warnings at the Zion Canyon Visitor Center before your hike.

Zion Canyon's Riverside Walk, which starts at the Temple of Sinawava, takes visitors through a pleasant wetland area along the Virgin River.

Hikers venture into **The Narrows** at the end of Riverside Walk

Zion-Mount Carmel Highway

The Great Arch

Although most park visitors enter from the south, there is another, equally scenic way to arrive at Zion Canyon. The Zion-Mount Carmel Highway starts in Utah's high mesa country east of the park, descending almost 2,000 feet (610 m) to the floor of Zion Canyon. Along the way, travelers are treated to glimpses of spectacular scenery. Multi-hued sandstone formations, like sand dunes frozen in time, rise up on either side of the road. The formations glow red, orange, and yellow, contrasting with the blue desert sky above. Checkerboard Mesa is a good place to stop for photos. Its colorful weathered sandstone has eroded crosshatches running across its face.

After a popular one-mile (1.6-km) roundtrip hike to gawk at Canyon Overlook, visitors can drive their cars directly through a canyon wall. The Zion-Mount Carmel Tunnel was opened in 1930 to promote travel to the park. It cost nearly $2 million, took three years to build, and claimed the lives of two construction workers. It plunges 1.1 miles (1.8 km) into the cliff wall. During the dark passage through the tunnel, six large openings are broken out of the rock, revealing breathtaking views of the canyon far below.

After exiting the tunnel, the road winds down to the floor of Zion Canyon, first passing by Pine Creek Canyon and The Great Arch. This 400-foot (122-m) high sandstone structure is called a blind arch because it is not free-standing. Instead, it is recessed into the red sandstone cliff.

The 1.1-mile (1.6 km) Zion–Mount Carmel Tunnel (above) was first opened in 1930 to promote travel to Zion National Park. Checkerboard Mesa (below) is an example of the weathered sandstone formations found along the Zion–Mount Carmel Highway.

Kolob Canyons

Kolob Arch

One of Zion National Park's lesser-known treasures is Kolob Canyons. It is located in the northwest part of the park, just off Interstate 15 between Salt Lake City, Utah, and Las Vegas, Nevada. It is one of the least visited parts of Zion, but has its own visitor center and network of hiking trails. The Kolob Canyons area is higher in elevation than the rest of Zion. More rain falls here, supporting coniferous forests and abundant wildlife.

Kolob Canyons Road takes visitors on a winding tour up into Taylor Creek Canyon. Several vistas along the way give glimpses of the jagged sandstone peaks and deep canyons that occupy the area. At Kolob Canyons Viewpoint, at the end of the 5-mile (8-km) scenic road, canyons and soaring red cliffs, hidden from the interstate, reveal themselves. A series of finger canyons, wide at the mouth and narrowing to deep slots in their upper reaches, stretch toward you like the hand of a giant resting on the earth. Hanging valleys are visible high above the canyon floor, with short-lived waterfalls plunging downward from them during heavy rainstorms.

Several trails venture into the Kolob Canyons area. One strenuous, but rewarding, trek is the 14-mile (23-km) roundtrip trail to Kolob Arch. At 310 feet (94 m) long, it is one of the longest free-standing natural arches in the world.

A hummingbird perched along the Taylor Creek Trail.

A lizard (above) suns itself on a rock deep in a canyon within the Kolob Canyons section of Zion National Park. Higher in elevation, this part of the park gets more rain than Zion Canyon. Finger canyons (below) stretch out toward Kolob Canyons Viewpoint.

Future Challenges

Shuttle busses

Zion National Park receives more than 2.5 million visitors each year. Until recently, traffic congestion was very bad inside Zion Canyon, adding an unacceptable amount of noise, overcrowding, and pollution. Today, cars are no longer allowed from spring through autumn. Instead, the National Park Service added a system of propane-fueled shuttle busses to transport visitors up the canyon.

The free shuttle system runs from the town of Springdale, just outside the park, all the way up Zion Canyon to the Temple of Sinawava, with many stops along the way. The Park Service reports that each full shuttle replaces 28 cars and all the noise and pollution they bring. Since starting the shuttle bus system in 2000, traffic jams, air and noise pollution, stress, and damage to the landscape has been greatly reduced. A sense of quiet has returned to the canyon. People genuinely enjoy watching the beautiful scenery roll by as someone else does the driving for them.

Besides man-made headaches, Mother Nature also causes problems inside the park. In addition to the ever-present danger of flash flooding and landslides, wildfires are another challenge. Over the past 150 years, fires have usually been suppressed on federal lands. But in the long term, fire is good for the health of the forest ecosystem. It allows plant species to regenerate and recycles needed nutrients into the soil.

Unfortunately, past fire suppression policies have allowed dead material to accumulate on the forest floors. When finally ignited, often by lightning, these fires are much more severe, damaging trees and plants that otherwise would have survived a smaller forest fire. Today, the National Park Service, together with the National Forest Service, runs a fire management program that aims to keep park visitors and buildings safe, yet allows fire to do its job in maintaining the health of the forests in Zion National Park.

Quiet, propane-powered shuttle busses whisk park visitors through Zion Canyon (above). According to the National Park Service, each full bus replaces the noise and pollution of approximately 28 cars. A firefighter (below) douses flames in a canyon in Zion National Park.

Glossary

ECOSYSTEM

A biological community of animals, plants, and bacteria, all of whom live together in the same physical or chemical environment.

FEDERAL LANDS

Much of America's land, especially in the western part of the country, is maintained by the United States federal government. These are public lands owned by all U.S. citizens. There are many kinds of federal lands. National parks, like Zion National Park, are federal lands that are set aside so that they can be preserved. Other federal lands, such as national forests or national grasslands, are used in many different ways, including logging, ranching, and mining. Much of the land surrounding Zion National Park is maintained by the government, including several national forests and wildlife refuges.

FOREST SERVICE

The United States Department of Agriculture (USDA) Forest Service was started in 1905 to manage public lands in national forests and grasslands. The Forest Service today oversees an area of 191 million acres (77.3 million hectares), which is an amount of land about the same size as Texas. In addition to protecting and managing America's public lands, the Forest Service also conducts forestry research and helps many state government and private forestry programs.

MESA

A mesa is a small, high plateau or flat land with very steep sides. Mesas are common in the American Southwest. Many can be seen in Zion National Park.

MOUNTAIN MAN

An early explorer who lived in the largely unexplored mountainous areas of the American and Canadian West. Many mountain men earned a living by fur trapping and trading with Native Americans.

PLATEAU

A large, level area of elevated landscape.

SANDSTONE

A sedimentary rock made of sand or quartz grains. Usually, sandstone is created when layers of sediments pile up on the ocean floor and compress over millions of years, cementing the grains together. When the oceans recede, or when forces under the earth push the land up, the sandstone is revealed. The red, yellow, and brown rocks and cliffs of Zion National Park are mostly sandstone.

WETLAND

A wetland, sometimes called riparian, is an area of land that usually has standing water for most of the year, like swamps or marshes. Many wetlands have been set aside as preserves for wildlife. Many kinds of birds and animals depend on this habitat for nesting, food, and shelter.

Above: The evening sun lights up the cliffs along the entrance to Zion Canyon.

Index